Timeless Shore

Timeless Shores

Timeless Shores

Copyright © 2020 by Sue Wood
All rights reserved.

This book or any portion thereof may not be reproduced or used in any manner whatsoever without the express written permission from the author except for the use of brief excerpts in a book review.

Printed in the United Kingdom

First Printing, 2020

ISBN 9798616110480

Timeless Shores

by

Sue Wood

Dedication

I dedicate this book to my parents.

Derick, my father who took me blackberry picking and pond dipping and started my love of nature.
Eleanor, my mother who inspired me to follow my dreams.

Acknowledgements

I would like to thank the following friends and family for their help and support

Dale Kendrick for his editing skills

Warren Wood, Jill Simpson and Kim Louise for their continual support

Warren Wood, Jill Simpson and Kersty Lockhart for their photographs.

Robyn and Erika for their love of nature.

Timeless Shores

CONTENTS

1	Atlantic Storm	11
2	Donald's House	13
3	Falaisg	15
4	The Fireside	17
5	Oronsay	19
6	A Skye Midsummer Night	21
7	Mystical Bay	23
8	River Roskhill in Spate	25
9	Western Sunset	27
10	Distant Isle	29
11	Driftwood	30
12	Wilderness	33
13	Wild Glen	35
14	Two Sister's Croft House	37
15	Down to the Shore	39
16	Dark, Dark Sky	41
17	Through the Old Gate	43
18	The Rowan Tree	45
19	Curlew calling	47
20	MacLeod's View	49
21	Thistles	51
22	Silent Pool	53

Timeless Shores

23	Fairy pools	55
24	Shepherd Seamus	57
25	Island Shore	59
26	The Window of Time	60
27	Crofter Angus	63
28	Haiku Poems	65
29	Atlantic Ocean	67
30	Cuillin Mountains	69
31	The Burn	71
32	Isle of Skye	73
33	Blowing a Hooley	75
34	Highland Cattle	77
35	Midge Marauders	79
37	Single Track Road	81
38	The Bothy	83
39	Harbour seals	85
40	Neist Point Lighthouse	87
41	Skye Skies	89
42	Talisker Bay	91
43	The Broch	93
44	Calluna	95
45	Piper's Cave	97
46	Ceilidh	99
47	Illustrations	100
49	About the Author	103

Timeless Shores

Timeless Shores

Timeless Shores

Atlantic Storm

Blasting the isle with caustic brine,

Wave upon wave, time after time.

Thunderous guns, quake the soul,

Defeating your foe with a ruthless goal.

Mighty rollers batter the shore,

Dousing the land, 'til it cries No more!

You show no mercy for boats and trees,

Lashing their forms with swollen seas.

Beasts and men hide from your raid,

Until you ebb and your forces fade.

Serenity and peace, the isle is still,

Carnage strewn from your barbarous will.

The seas are calm with gentle tides

We surface then and leave our hides.

Skye survives your brutal assail,

The land, the lochs, the hills prevail.

Timeless Shores

Donald's House

The luminous walls glow in the moonlight,

Gable window flickers, with orange delight.

Smoke plumes rise from the chimney stack,

Charred wood aroma, called us back.

Memories of relaxing in front of the fire,

Little more bliss did we desire.

Watching the flames' spiralling dance,

Glowing faces in a spellbound trance.

Savouring a dram with joyful craic,

These times, sadly

will not come back.

Timeless Shores

Falaisg

Days are longer, Spring is near,

Time for falaisg, the start of the year.

Crofters await a time without rain,

To light the fires, flickering flame.

The plume rises and covers the land,

In smothering smoke, a hazy band.

Lapping flames with orange glow,

Spread through the night, an amber flow.

A wonderous scene to see at night,

Warms our thoughts at the vivid sight.

A pleasant aroma fills the air,

While Crofter's labour at, this time of year.

Clearing the ground, improving the graze,

A Springtime custom, and a welcome blaze.

(falaisg-moor burning)

The Fireside

There's a pleasing warmth, inside the soul,

While watching the flames flicker and glow.

The bursting embers crackle and flare,

As purple flames suddenly appear.

Imagined faces and shapes to see,

On the burning logs from the old tree.

This focal point with aesthetic lure,

Holds our gaze to this sight, so pure.

The heat embraces and warms our form,

Releasing tensions like, ebbing storms.

At evenings end we sadly retire,

Leaving this wonderful friendly fire.

Timeless Shores

Oronsay

This isle is a wonderful calming place,

With soothing waves, big skies and space.

Who has passed these timeless shores?

On Long ships, Whalers, Creelers and more.

Distant lands beckon and call

To offer new lives to one and all.

A sweet girl dreams of her special beau,

What is their future? Only time will show.

A young man dreams of a life at sea,

Ten years from now, where will he be?

Sons and daughters have sailed away,

Though their hearts will always stay.

A mother prays for her men to come home,

Waiting in anguish, silently alone.

This Isle comforts and allays our fears,

Our troubled minds it heals and clears.

Time will pass and lives will alter,

This isle of dreams will never falter.

Timeless Shores

Skye Midsummer Night

The mirrored loch reflects the light,

With magenta tones glowing bright,

As wispy mist swirls from the land

And oyster catchers preen on the sand.

The curlew glides low as he sings,

His melodious air, as if to bring

The promise of dawn in the fading light

On this glorious eve of midsummer night.

Timeless Shores

Mystical Bay

I walk up the lane where the cattle lie low,

And follow the track where the green ferns grow.

Heather and bracken beneath my feet,

Puddles and streams coloured with peat.

Splatters of mud speckle my garb,

With clicks and jags from briars' barb.

As foliage clears, a breath-taking scene,

Opens up the world with a vision, serene.

Surrounded by crags, cliffs and the sea

Overwhelms my senses and makes me feel free.

I descend on the shore, to this eerie place,

With mystical feelings of solace and grace.

Upon the rise, through the flags of gold,

Three sacred graves of granite unfold.

Facing the sea, a comfort they sought,

The trio of graves, prompts reflection and thought.

This sacred place so tranquil and pure,

A mystical bay, with great allure.

Timeless Shores

River Roskhill in Spate

Your turbulent floods hide rocks and rises,

Take all in your wake, which never surprises.

I watch with wonder and feel your power,

Making a spectacle from a torrential shower.

Diamonds rise from your liquid gold,

Such a wondrous sight to behold.

Thundering down the gorge with force,

The dominance you hold, we can only endorse.

Saplings of rowan bow and curtsy to you,

As they succumb and you take them from view.

You rage and you roar with a ferocious sound,

A natural phenomenon, your show does astound.

Timeless Shores

Western Sunset

On this amazing eve, with air so still,

I watch in wonder at this sight to thrill.

My visual senses watch colours ablaze,

Sun sinking down in a dramatic haze.

Merging pinks with fading gold,

Colours so vibrant and hues so bold,

Light up the sky and create a show

Of mountains and hills, mauve they glow.

Islands afar, in shades of grey,

Entice to embark, discover and stay.

Peace and pleasure fill the mind,

With aesthetic bliss, a vision refined.

Timeless Shores

Distant Isle

The tranquil waves shimmer and flow,

Beneath blue-sky's iridescent glow.

Streaks of silver appear and fade

With dark cobalt and brilliant jade.

This aqua flow of changing light

Mirrors the luminous sky, so bright.

And in the distance an island lies;

Within a sea of restless tides.

The isle is grey with amethyst hues,

Pristine shores and stunning views

I long to visit this arcane place,

Its rocky crags, seascapes and space.

Driftwood

Floating and swirling, wishing to flee,

How many years have you been at sea?

Washed upon shores, abandoned on sands,

Restless tides and distant lands.

Battered by storms in different seas,

You cannot be tamed because, you are free.

Your battles and torments have shaped your form,

Enduring all, you await the next storm.

Longing for peace and a time to hide,

But storms and demons, you must abide.

Timeless Shores

Hope at last, a friendly shore,

Though besieged you must, explore.

Lower your guard and finally trust,

Unburden your mind, a time to adjust.

Take tentative steps on your fragile earth,

Lose anger, anxiety, shame and low worth.

Feel the release of the crushing weight,

You now control your future fate.

Calming seas, blue skies and sun,

Your future is bright,

Your battle is won.

Timeless Shores

Wilderness

Thunderous clouds are gathering on high,

While golden eagles screech out their cry.

Ominous mountains dominate the land,

Enormous statues; colossal they stand.

The ravens circle and rattle their call,

As they rise on the thermals before they fall.

Scots pines are arched from constant storms,

Tortured and sculpted in twisted forms.

Wild willows yield to the western gales

Whipping their branches; leaving them frail.

A wild place of freedom; a site to hide,

Where powerful raptors hunt and reside.

Timeless Shores

Wild Glen

Far in the distance lies a secret glen
Untamed and wild, not seen by men.
The mountains are high on every side,
Deep, secret glen colossal and wide.
The harts and hinds have ruled at will,
Thousands of years they've roamed these hills.
Foreboding crags bear down from high,
Ominous clouds in thunderous skies.
Untainted land which, should be feared.
This sacred ground must be revered.

Timeless Shores

Two Sister's Croft House

The small grey house with the flaking door,

And gossamer panes hiding rooms to explore.

A crack in the gable where water seeps,

Bulging walls where green ivy creeps.

The lean-to shed with the slamming door,

A life time's belongings, in use, no more.

Numerous roof tiles scattered around,

Like slate-grey diamonds, peppering the ground.

The two sister's croft house, a home no more,

…But waiting for someone to love and restore.

Timeless Shores

Down to the Shore

Golden grass feathers brush passed my knees,

As I walk down the path which, leads to the sea.

Soft downy thistles float on the air,

My mood is bright, without a care.

The rocks are patterned with lichen lace,

As the sun shines down to warm my face.

Sapphire sparkles glint in the rays,

On this glorious morning; this beautiful day.

The sand is warm between my toes,

While swirling water ebbs and flows.

The salty scent drifts on the breeze,

This calming shore; I feel so at ease.

Timeless Shores

Dark, Dark Skies

Jet-black ink fills the sky

Complete darkness as, I look up high.

Nothing to see, a total black void.

Until the darkness reveals the joy.

Of a million stars, shining on high,

Minute sparkles adorning the sky.

No orange glow from urban sprawl,

A vast black canopy; amazing to all.

Timeless Shores

Through the Old Gate

Through the old gate, which leads to the moor,

Is a wilderness, vast and pure.

A windy track weaves up the rise,

With heather and moss on every side.

Upon the rise, I hear the larks' choir,

Which fills the air, with tunes to inspire.

I dip to the low ground, on moss of green,

Which oozes water, translucent and clean.

Two burns merge on the lower ground,

Burbling and gurgling, with a calming sound.

I rise again towards the brown crags

Where the grass is strewn with yellow flags.

I find a rock to sit on and rest,

And breathe sweet air as I look to the west.

I observe the mountains rising high,

MacLeod's tables, against the sky.

This wonderful place, is a gift to us all,

Drawing us back with its wilderness call

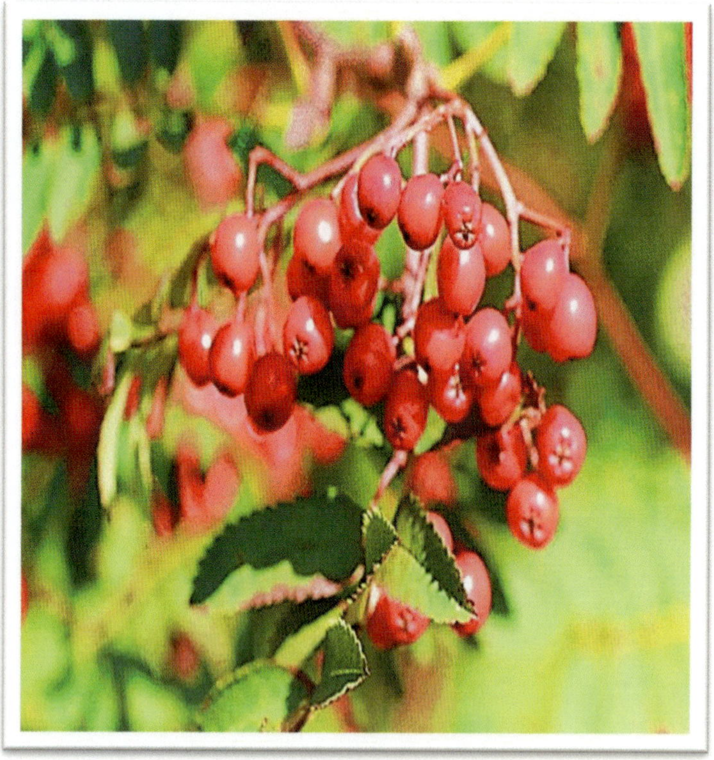

The Rowan Tree

Glorious and graceful, with a striking pose,

From a tiny seed you grew and rose.

Delicate leaves like friendly hands,

Wave to all who watch and stand.

Clusters of flowers, with scents so sweet,

Fill the air with a fragrant treat.

Berries like rubies, red with a shine,

Nourish the birds, throughout Autumn time.

An Autumn special show, you share,

And a stunning time, we await each year.

Celtic myths you bring to our lives,

The tree of life, which makes us wise.

Guarding our families from evil, your goal,

And making us brave to complete your role.

The tree of life so strong and tall,

A seasonal beauty, captivating us all.

Timeless Shores

Curlew Calling

Across the moor where the land is wild,
Bog cotton and reeds on every side.
Wind swept and fresh, with freedom to roam,
Solitude and peace away from home.
Rest in stillness, a solitary time,
The world is calm, a moment so fine.
The silence is broken, with a haunting cry,
A curious call with a pitch, so high.
An eerie song from a distant rise,
Curlew calling, the song of the wild.
Mysterious and haunting, music to love,
A beguiling silhouette, glides above.
He searches the moor for a suitable site,
To build a nest in a place just right.
Again, he calls to his mate close by,
A courtship ritual as they soar and fly.
Early Spring, this time of year,
Curlews delight with their song, they share.

Timeless Shores

MacLeod's View

The castle turrets are a perfect site,

To view the loch with its vibrant light.

Turquoise sea peppered with isles,

A magical vision which, spreads for miles.

Dunvegan Head with its cliffs so steep,

Repel the tides and waves which weep.

The seaweed clings to the friendly rocks,

Orange-brown lace, like, dancing frocks.

MacLeod's tables stand up on high,

Ancient summits against the sky,

Clouds race by in their sky of blue,

Enriching this vista of MacLeod's view.

Timeless Shores

Thistles

Majestic crowns, no blooms could surpass,

Standing tall above feathery grass

Bright emerald-green colouring their leaves

And spiky thorns which wind and weave.

At Summer's end they fade and die

Dispersing seeds to float on high.

They rest on the ground and wait all year,

When their blossom's burst without a care.

They adorn the land with purple light,

A Summertime show of floral delight.

Timeless Shores

Silent Pool

Rain shower rivulets collect on the moor,
Making puddles and streams, clean and pure.
Twisting and flowing across the ground,
A fluid cascade with a blissful sound.
Cool crystal liquid of amber and gold
Collect in the river, a sight to behold.
Gurgling downhill with speedy flight,
Over rocks and rapids, frothy and white.
Slowing now, through the lower ground,
Quiet and calm, with a gentle sound.
Water so still and liquid so cool,
Lies the glass mirror, the silent pool.
Reflecting the ferns and lichen behind,
A colourful image, of nature, refined.
A film adorned with ripples and rings,
This glistening liquor is shimmering.
The silent pool, which gives great ease,
From troubled lives, our mind it frees.

Timeless Shores

Fairy Pools

Beneath the Black Cuillin is a special place;
Translucent mirror which shimmers with grace.
Ripples and rings, shining so bright
Reflect the suns' rays with diamond light.
Turquoise and clear this water so cool.
Enticing to all, this pure fairy pool.
This spuming cascade has played so long,
Filling the air with music and song.
Pure clean air to breathe then…sigh…
Precious moments as time passes by.
The Cuillin's look down and perceive the flow,
Of the fairy pools with unearthly glow.

Timeless Shores

Shepherd Seamus

Sauntering across the moor with ease,
Silver-grey hair blows in the breeze.
Billowing coat with dark tanned skin,
Chiselled jaw with a playful grin.
Sheepskin waistcoat with leather lace,
Character lines criss-cross his face.
With Meg at heal and crook in hand,
He scans the park: his treasured land.
Shearing done, he carries a fleece,
Heading for home for a dram,
In peace.

Timeless Shores

Island Shore

Gentle breeze, cooling the skin,

The turquoise glass is shimmering.

Lapping waves on the pebble band,

Tides ebbing flow, with fizzing sand.

Mother of pearl on spiralling winkles,

Adorn the shore with glossy sprinkles.

Rippling sand, with ridges and dips,

A bubbling stream, swirls and twists.

The Oystercatcher calls the alarm,

Her scurrying chicks, hide from harm.

Seagulls bob on the rippling brine,

With five or more in a jagged line.

Golden glow of coral sand meets,

The crisp high tides brittle band.

Salty air, refreshing this place,

A natural vista and flawless space.

The Window of Time

A young mother sits nursing her child,

Her lullaby song is gentle and mild.

She awaits her man's return from sea.

Their precious son at last he will see.

Timeless Shores

The children laugh and play on the floor,
Their yearly growth is, etched on the door.
How they have grown! In the blink of an eye,
Away from the nest they soon must fly.

The children have left to start new lives,
Chose mainland folk for husbands and wives.
They visit each Summer, a blissful time,
Her wonderful family; a visit sublime.

Aged eighty-nine, she watches the rain,
Through the sash window's cloudy pane.
She's proud of her time a good mother and wife,
Thinking back with a smile;
On a wonderful life.

Timeless Shores

Crofter Angus

Three scores and ten he's worked this land,

As both granddad and father; he lent a hand.

The tatties are growing in ten straight lines,

A crofter's chore near Easter time.

The peats are in and drying fine,

A vital fuel through Winter time.

His oilcloth coat tied up with rope,

Hangs on the nail (to dry, he hopes)

The peaty Rayburn smokes and spits,

His favourite chair, he eases and sits.

He savours a dram with closing eyes,

Looks back on his life,

Oh… how time flies!

Timeless Shores

Haiku Poems

Timeless Shores

Atlantic Ocean

Ocean tides begin

with the drawing from the moon

ending on our shores

Timeless Shores

Cuillin Mountains

The mountains stand tall,

watching the land stretching far,

guarding their kingdom.

Timeless Shores

The Burn

The fast burn sprays bronze

Over rocks, rises and dips

For eternity.

Timeless Shores

Isle of Skye

Mountains, lochs and moors,

wild landscapes and open skies,

pure clean air to breathe.

Timeless Shores

Blowing a Hooley

Horizontal rain,

buckling trees bend and snap,

as the wild wind howls.

Timeless Shores

Highland Cattle

Wild shaggy cattle,

wide eyes and ferocious horns,

magnificent beasts.

Timeless Shores

Midge Marauders

Midges swarm in clouds,

waiting to pounce on their prey

best run for cover.

Timeless Shores

Single Track

Scenic winding roads,

passing place stand offs

aplenty,

who will reverse first?

Timeless Shores

The Bothy

The old stone bothy,

gives shelter and a lifeline

to lost travellers

Timeless Shores

Harbour Seals

Their deep soulful eyes,

watching the expanse of ocean,

dreaming of their prey.

Timeless Shores

Neist Point Lighthouse

Skye's westerly point,

shining into the dark night,

guiding ships back home.

Timeless Shores

Skye Skies

Vast magical skies,

envelop this Misty Isle,

constantly changing.

Timeless Shores

Talisker Bay

Vast skies and open seas,

black stack dominates the view,

a sentry on watch.

Timeless Shores

The Broch

Standing tall above,

the lochs, lands and people

an ancient beacon.

Timeless Shores

Calluna

Rich purple colours

Blanket the hills in Summer

Sweet heavenly scent

Timeless Shores

Piper's Cave

Beneath the sheer cliffs

Lies the secret piper's cave

A peaceful haven

Timeless Shores

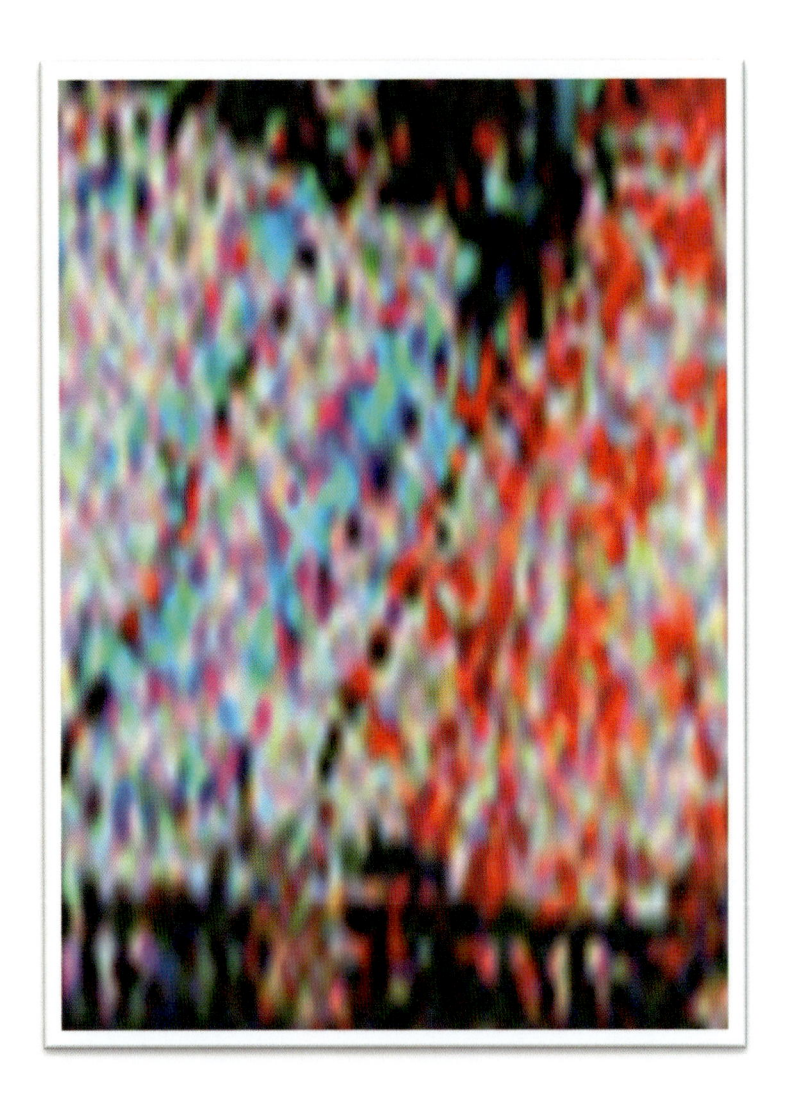

Ceilidh

Spinning and twirling

Pipers and fiddlers playing

Exhilaration!

Illustrations and Images

1	Atlantic Storm SW art	10
2	Donald's House SW art	12
3	Falaisg SW art	14
4	The Fireside SW photo	16
5	Oronsay KL photo	18
6	Skye Midsummer Night SW art	20
7	Coral Beach SW photo	22
8	River Roskhill in Spate SW photo	24
9	Western Sunset SW art	26
10	Loch Bracadale SW photo	28
11	Driftwood SW art	30
12	Camasunary SW photo	32
13	Cuillin Range KL photo	34
14	Old Croft House SW photo	36
15	Flowers & Loch Dunvegan SW photo	38
16	Starry Sky SW art	40
17	Old Gate, Roskhill SW photo	42
18	Rowan Berries WW photo	44
19	Curlew in Flight SW art	46
20	Loch Dunvegan SW photo	48
21	Thistles SW photo	50

Timeless Shores

22	River Roskhill SW photo	52
23	Cascade SW art	54
24	Shepherd Ian SW art	56
25	Island Shore SW art	58
27	Old Window SW photo	60
28	Crofter SW photo	62
29	Haiku Poems SW art	65
30	Atlantic Ocean SW art	63
31	Cuillin Mountains SW photo	68
32	Highland Burn SW photo	70
33	MacLeod's Tables SW photo	72
34	Stormy Tree SW art	74
35	Highland Cow SW photo	76
36	Midge Swarm SW art	78
37	Claigan Road, Skye SW photo	80
38	Old croft House SW art	82
39	Harbour Seals SW photo	84
40	Neist Point Lighthouse SW photo	86
41	Skye Sunrise KL photo	88
42	Talisker Bay SW photo	90
43	Dun Beag Broch, Struan SW photo	92
44	Calluna Heather SW photo	94
45	Cave Glendale Beach SW photo	96
46	Ceilidh Dance SW art	98
47	Author	103

Timeless Shores

About the Author

I grew up in England and was fortunate enough to live in an area surrounded by farmland and open spaces. My childhood was packed full of outdoor play; building camps, making mud pies, creating perfume from rose petals and having lots of freedom. My environment was full of the natural world with an abundance of birds, beetles and wild flowers. My Father took me and my siblings blackberry picking and pond dipping on a regular basis. These were very happy times, which gave me the love of nature; a happy place to enjoy and feel at home in. In so many ways this was an idyllic childhood, which is now quite scarce. It was a magical time and enhanced my fascination with the natural world, which provided an environment to recharge my batteries during some difficult times. Nature is perfect for improving mental health and putting things into perspective.

Throughout my career I have always worked with pre-school children in education settings and with students in further education. I completed Child and Youth studies to gain my degree and followed this with a diploma in teaching in further education. I was a lecturer for the University of Highlands and Islands (UHI) teaching both school leavers and mature students in Portree. My main focus throughout my career has been to promote the importance of the natural world for children's happiness, health and wellbeing. Once children have been fully engaged into the natural world, they will take this forward into adulthood. This is a wonderful gift, which is a natural tonic and can help protect physical and mental health for life. Currently, I am fortunate to work in Dunvegan primary school with local children and families.

I first visited Skye in the 1980's with my husband Warren and I will never forget this magical time of crystal-clear lochs, dramatic mountains and beautiful scenery. We arrived on a sunny afternoon and met Seamus the shepherd who gave us directions in typical Skye banter. We also met a wonderful couple called Cal and Marie from Borreraig, who welcomed us with open arms. We eventually made the decision to move to Skye in 1993, when the children were still young. It took a further two years to come to fruition, but … we did it! Moving to Skye with my husband and young family was a "dream come true". To be surrounded by the wonderful environment of this dramatic landscape, with its abundance of wildlife, was amazing.

We have lived on Skye for 25 years and we are now fortunate to have a croft, which we acquired four years ago. The croft has a wildflower meadow adjacent to the banks of the river Roskhill. I named this meadow Òran Uisge (Song of Water) because, while sitting amongst the wild flowers, the river gently flows along, towards the sea, providing a tranquil sound. Òran Uisge is an inspirational place to watch the bees and butterflies foraging for food, enjoying fragrance from the wildflowers filling the air and listen to the abundance of songbirds. This inspired me to create skyenatureblog.com which, provides a selection of posts with poems, artwork, nature quotes, photographs and videos all relating to this inspirational island. This wonderful setting also inspired me to write my first poem "*Skye Midsummer Night*", followed by "*The Silent Pool*". I continued to write and decided to publish them in my first book "*Timeless Shores*"

A percentage from each book sale will be donated to mental health charities on Skye.

Timeless Shores

Timeless Shores

Printed in Great Britain
by Amazon